DUDLEY SCHOOLS
LIBRARY SERVICE

The Shang Dynasty

Written by Anna Claybourne

Contents

D1610052

Schools Library and Information Services

S00000783293

Dragon bones

In 1899, a Chinese man called Wang Yirong
bought some "dragon bones". These weren't
really from dragons – people just called them that,
as dragons often feature in Chinese legends.
They were old cow bones and tortoise shells,
found in farmers' fields. People used to grind
them up to use as medicine.

Wang Yirong was an expert in Chinese alphabets,
and he noticed that the bones were carved
with ancient writing. Wang died soon after this,
but other experts began to study the writing
on the bones. They found it was about
the kings of the Shang dynasty, who lived in
China 3,000 years earlier.

Until then, no one knew if the Shang had really existed.
They were mentioned in old history books,
but many people thought they were legendary,
like ancient Greek gods. The bones showed
they were real people – the first Chinese
people to write their history down.

The dragon bones are now called "oracle bones". This one is a cow's shoulder blade.

Who were the Shang?

The Shang people lived in what is now northern China, in and around the Yellow River valley. The Shang dynasty, or series of rulers, lasted from the 1600s BCE until 1046 BCE – a period of over 500 years.

The Yellow River is one of China's biggest rivers. It provided water, which the Shang needed for their crops and animals, as well as for themselves. It was also a transport route for boats. The Shang civilisation and its cities were located around the river.

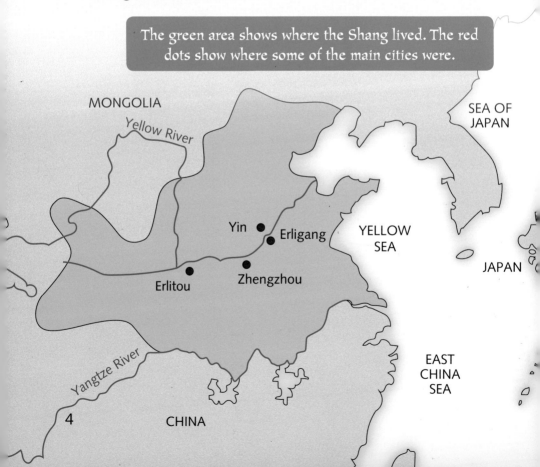

The green area shows where the Shang lived. The red dots show where some of the main cities were.

MONGOLIA

Yellow River

SEA OF JAPAN

Yin

Erligang

YELLOW SEA

JAPAN

Erlitou

Zhengzhou

Yangtze River

EAST CHINA SEA

4

CHINA

The Shang dynasty is divided into three main eras or time periods, based on where the capital city was at the time:

- the Erlitou, from 1600–1500 BCE

- the Erligang, from about 1500–1300 BCE

- the Anyang or Yinxu, from 1300–1050 BCE: this is the one we know most about, as the oracle bones date from this time.

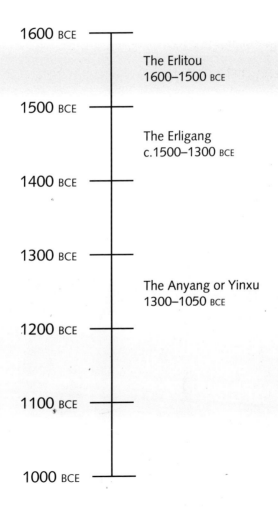

1600 BCE	
	The Erlitou 1600–1500 BCE
1500 BCE	
	The Erligang c.1500–1300 BCE
1400 BCE	
1300 BCE	
	The Anyang or Yinxu 1300–1050 BCE
1200 BCE	
1100 BCE	
1000 BCE	

The Shang was a very ancient civilisation. They lived more than 3,000 years ago – much longer ago than the great age of ancient Greece, or the Roman Empire.

While Shang kings ruled in China, the pharaohs were ruling ancient Egypt, the Olmec people were in Mexico, and the Bronze-Age people in Europe had recently finished building Stonehenge.

For a long time, we only knew about the Shang from the writings of Chinese historians, such as Sima Qian, who lived over 2,100 years ago, around 100 BCE. His work includes many details about Shang kings. When experts **decoded** the writing on the oracle bones, they were amazed to find the information on them closely matched the history books, even though they had been written long after Shang times.

Stonehenge is a huge stone monument in England, built several thousand years ago.

Since then, **archaeologists** have uncovered the remains of Shang cities, workshops, palaces and houses. They've also found ancient Shang tombs full of bronze treasures, money, weapons and everyday items. From all this, we can piece together how the Shang lived.

An archaeologist explores the remains of a Shang dynasty chariot and its two horses.

Shang kings

The Shang dynasty was ruled by a long line of kings.
When a king died, power was handed down to the next oldest
son in the ruling family. That could mean the king's own son,
or sometimes one of his brothers or a nephew. There were
no female monarchs. Many periods in Chinese history are
named after their ruling dynasty, such as the Qin, Han and
Ming dynasties.

This tomb in Beijing pays respect
to the Ming dynasty.

There were about 30 Shang kings altogether. The records sometimes disagree about when each king ruled, and how long for. But we know quite a lot about some of them, such as Wu Ding, who was on the throne for 58 years from 1250–1192 BCE, and the last Shang king, Di Xin, who ruled for almost 30 years, from 1075–1046 BCE.

This decorated bronze cauldron dates from the reign of the Shang king Wu Ding.

Shang society

If you lived in Shang times, you knew your place! Everyone had their own position in society, and had to stick to their role.

Royals and nobles

At the top were the royal family, and the nobles, who were often related to them. They were very rich. As well as ruling, they spent their time fighting battles against enemies, going hunting and holding religious **rituals**.

Fact file: Royal names

Only the royals and nobles had surnames. This meant they were the only ones who could trace their family line and worship their ancestors.
This was an important part of Shang religion.

The rich royals and nobles owned valuable items, like this carved ivory vase.

Commoners

Most people were commoners, and had a variety of jobs.
A lot were farmers, but there were also builders, bronze
workers, carvers, potters, silk weavers, cooks and many more
skilled workers.

Slaves

Experts think the Shang also kept slaves to do the hardest work.
These were often prisoners who had been captured from
other kingdoms. Some of them ended up being used for
human **sacrifices**.

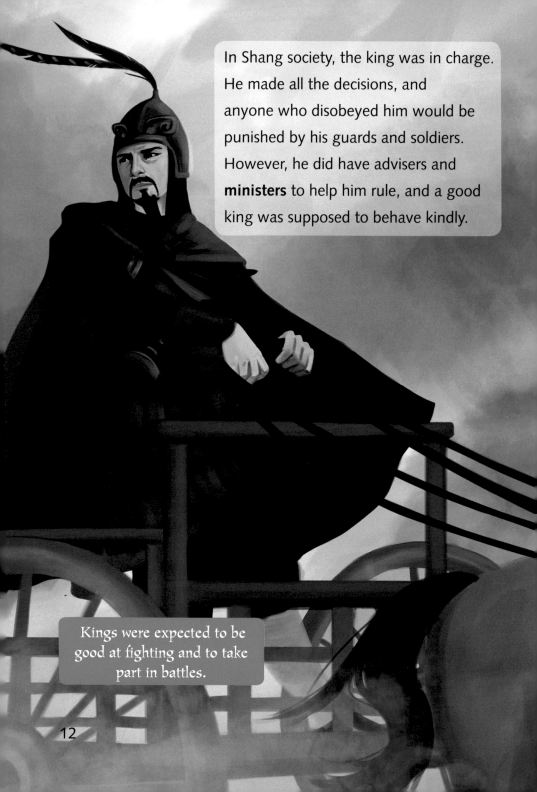

In Shang society, the king was in charge. He made all the decisions, and anyone who disobeyed him would be punished by his guards and soldiers. However, he did have advisers and **ministers** to help him rule, and a good king was supposed to behave kindly.

Kings were expected to be good at fighting and to take part in battles.

If anyone tried to overthrow the king, he could use his armies to defeat them. Kings often led their armies into battle themselves.

It was a bad idea to be an enemy of the Shang, as they were so powerful. Rulers of nearby kingdoms would visit the Shang king with gifts, to show they wanted to be friends.

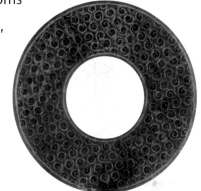

Kings gave their nobles carved jade discs like this as a symbol of their role. The jade discs could be the size of a doughnut or even a small plate.

VIP file: King Wu Yi

Wu Yi ruled for 35 years from 1147-1112 BCE. According to Chinese historians, he was very **arrogant** and loved showing off. He made a puppet of a Shang god, then made it "lose" at games to show he was better than the gods. Wu Yi died when he went on a hunting trip and was struck by lightning! This was seen as a punishment from heaven.

Women in the Shang dynasty

For the Shang, men were more important than women. Having a baby boy was seen as a success, while having a girl was a let-down. For example, the writing on one oracle bone asks whether the king's wife will have a "good" birth. The oracle bone also gives the results: "She gave birth; it was not good. It was a girl."

Shang kings often had several wives. They could play a big role by advising the king, or taking part in religious ceremonies. Sometimes, the wives competed over whose son would be the next king, as this was one way women could win respect.

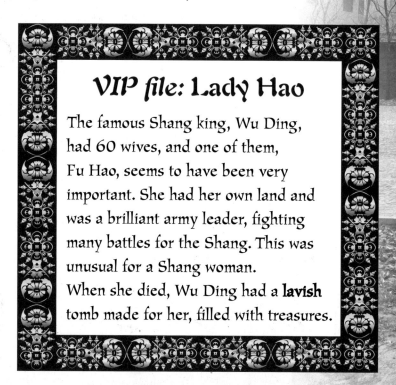

VIP file: Lady Hao

The famous Shang king, Wu Ding, had 60 wives, and one of them, Fu Hao, seems to have been very important. She had her own land and was a brilliant army leader, fighting many battles for the Shang. This was unusual for a Shang woman.

When she died, Wu Ding had a **lavish** tomb made for her, filled with treasures.

This modern statue of the warrior queen Lady Fu Hao stands near her tomb in Yinxu.

What did the Shang believe?

Shang religion was based on gods, **ancestors** and a strong belief in the afterlife. According to legend, the Shang was once a clan ruled over by the ancient Xia dynasty. (Though ancient Chinese historians described the Xia, there's very little evidence of them.)

It was said that the Shang dynasty began with Shang leader Cheng Tang. He gained enough power to overthrow the merciless Xia emperor, King Jie, and became the first Shang king.

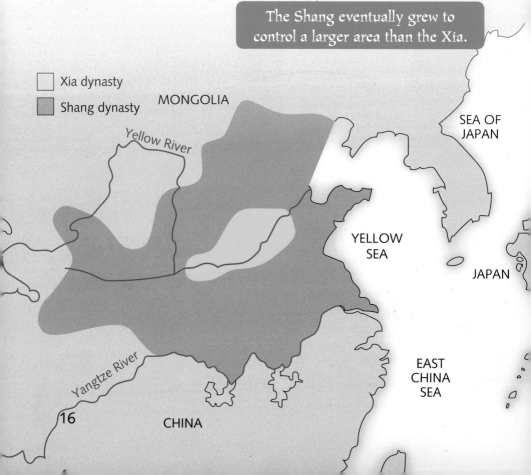

The Shang eventually grew to control a larger area than the Xia.

☐ Xia dynasty
◼ Shang dynasty

MONGOLIA

Yellow River

SEA OF JAPAN

YELLOW SEA

JAPAN

Yangtze River

EAST CHINA SEA

16

CHINA

VIP file: King Cheng Tang

Cheng Tang, the first Shang king, reigned in
the 1600s BCE. After the cruelty of King Jie, he tried
to rule wisely and kindly. He encouraged people to
be creative and bring him their ideas. After a severe
drought, he gave money to poor people to help them
survive. The Shang saw him as a perfect example of how
a king should behave.

Ancestors

The Shang worshipped their ancestors. This included previous kings and nobles, and sometimes their wives. The ancestors were thought to live in a spirit world, and could still influence events in the living world.

Priests and kings would sacrifice food and wine to the ancestors, in special bronze containers called "ding". They also sacrificed animals such as oxen and sheep. Sometimes, they sacrificed humans too – especially prisoners of war from other kingdoms.

This is the bronze head of an axe, probably used to behead sacrifice victims.

These are pottery models of war prisoners. Prisoners were likely to become human sacrifices as part of a Shang custom.

Gods

Besides the ancestors, the Shang had a supreme god, named Shangdi or Di. He was in charge of many other gods, who controlled things like war, weather and harvests. Shang priests and kings prayed to the ancestors to ask these gods to help them.

ding

Fact file: Ancestor worship

Worshipping ancestors is common in many cultures around the world, both past and present. Examples include the ancient Egyptians, the Celts, and the Magalasy people, who live in Madagascar in Africa.

Using the oracle bones

Oracle bones – the "dragon bones" that led to the discovery of Shang remains – were used to talk to the ancestors.

First, the flat piece of bone or tortoiseshell was scraped smooth, to make a good writing surface. Holes were drilled into the underside. Then a **scribe** would carve a question on to the bone. It could be something like, "Will we have success in battle tomorrow?" or "Are the ancestors causing the floods?"

The next part of the ceremony was to insert a heated metal stick into the holes in the bone. This would make it suddenly crack. From the way the bone cracked, a priest or king would **interpret** the ancestors' answer – often just "yes" or "no".

Later, a description of what actually happened – a battle defeat, for example – was added to the bone. As the bones also recorded the date and which king was in power, they provide a detailed record of Shang events.

This oracle bone is made from the shell and underside of a tortoise.

Burials and tombs

When a Shang king or noble died, they were buried in an elaborate tomb along with treasure, money, weapons and personal possessions. The Shang believed the person needed these things for the afterlife, when they would become an important ancestor.

Fu Hao's tomb, for example, contained dozens of bronze sacrifice bowls, pottery, stone ornaments, jade hair clips and combs, as well as her war weapons.

a jade comb

a finely carved jug

a container for warming wine in

Besides valuable objects, Shang tombs are also full of people! They were the dead person's servants, bodyguards and advisers, who'd also be needed in the next life. They were killed first or buried alive, along with slaves or prisoners who were sacrificed to the ancestors. The Shang also buried pet dogs and other animals with their owners.

Fact file: Everyday graves

If they didn't end up accompanying their boss into the tomb, commoners and slaves had a less grand burial. Their graves were usually just basic pits in the ground.

the tomb of Lady Fu Hao, with some of the objects that were found there

23

Life in the countryside

If you lived in the Shang dynasty, you'd probably be a farmer, as this is what most people spent their time doing.

The most important crop was millet, a type of grain. Farmers also grew wheat, rice, corn and barley, and kept cows, sheep and chickens. Horses and buffaloes pulled ploughs and carts.

Millet is still an important crop in many parts of the world.

The Yellow River valley was good for farming, with plenty of **fertile** soil. But the river could also cause disastrous flooding that could wash away crops and homes. Shang farmers built systems that channelled water away from the river, to water the fields while helping to prevent floods.

Disastrous floods still happen on the Yellow River.

What did they eat?

Most people lived on a type of milky porridge or stew, made from millet or other grains. They collected wild apricots, chestnuts and berries, and sometimes grew vegetables such as cucumbers. They also ate eggs and fish.

Commoners rarely ate meat themselves. They farmed animals for the king and nobles to eat, or to use in sacrifices.

People usually cooked
over a fire. They used
a type of three-legged
pot called a "li",
that could stand over
the flames, and another
pot with holes in
the bottom fitted on top,
for steaming food in.

a li

Fact file: Chopsticks

Chopsticks, used throughout China as an eating tool, first
appeared in the Shang dynasty. A bronze pair was found in
a Shang tomb, dating from about 1200 BCE (making them
over 3,200 years old!).

Silk and silkworms

Besides growing food, the Shang also farmed silk, which was already an important part of Chinese culture. Silk farmers fed silkworms on the leaves of the mulberry tree, and collected their cocoons. They wove the threads from the cocoons to make luxurious silk fabric for royalty and nobles to wear. As the dynasty went on, they developed ways of weaving beautiful patterns into the cloth. The Shang even had a god of silkworms!

a fragment of Shang Dynasty silk

This carved silkworm shows how important these insects were to the Shang.

Getting around

Ordinary people had to walk from A to B, especially in
the countryside. Some longer trips were made by boat or raft.
They were used to carry silk fabric and other goods, like grain,
from one city to another along the Yellow River. The Shang also
had horse-drawn carts and carriages. Shang kings rode into
battle on chariots.

Ornaments and models like this show how
some carts might have looked.

Buildings

The biggest city buildings were the royal palaces and temples. They were built by forming low walls out of packed-together earth, with a wooden frame on top and a thatched roof. Some smaller houses were built this way too.

However, many people in the city lived in a different kind of home – a carved-out cave. The ground in the Yellow River valley is made of a kind of soft rock called loess, which is easy to cut. People dug into it to make simple homes, using pillars to hold up the roof.

Some people in China still live in loess cave homes today.

Getting around

Ordinary people had to walk from A to B, especially in the countryside. Some longer trips were made by boat or raft. They were used to carry silk fabric and other goods, like grain, from one city to another along the Yellow River. The Shang also had horse-drawn carts and carriages. Shang kings rode into battle on chariots.

Ornaments and models like this show how some carts might have looked.

Life in the city

The Shang were the first Chinese people to build large, complex cities. During the dynasty, they built new cities and moved their capital several times.

Ao

The ruins of an early Shang city, possibly called Ao, have been found near Zhengzhou. This city was protected by huge earth **ramparts**. These surrounded the city in a rectangle shape, with gaps where gates might have been. It contained royal palaces, houses, pottery workshops and small farms.

Yin

The remains of the bigger, more recent city of Yin, the last Shang capital, lie near Anyang. This was where the first oracle bones were found. Since then, **excavations** have turned up thousands more bones, palaces and royal living areas, temples, tombs and bronze-making workshops.

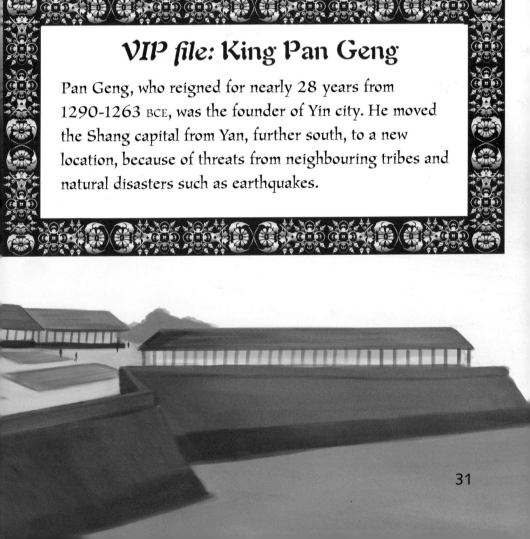

VIP file: King Pan Geng

Pan Geng, who reigned for nearly 28 years from 1290-1263 BCE, was the founder of Yin city. He moved the Shang capital from Yan, further south, to a new location, because of threats from neighbouring tribes and natural disasters such as earthquakes.

Buildings

The biggest city buildings were the royal palaces and temples.
They were built by forming low walls out of packed-together
earth, with a wooden frame on top and a thatched roof.
Some smaller houses were built this way too.

However, many people in the city lived in a different kind of
home – a carved-out cave. The ground in the Yellow River valley
is made of a kind of soft rock called loess, which is easy to cut.
People dug into it to make simple homes, using pillars to hold up
the roof.

Some people in China still live in
loess cave homes today.

Did the Shang have schools?

As far as experts can tell, Shang children didn't go to school. Royal and noble families may have had tutors to teach their children how to read and write, hunt and use weapons. Meanwhile, commoners would have copied their parents, or became apprentices, to learn skills like farming, carving or bronze casting.

It took years to learn to carve decorated jade items like this.

Military might

The Shang were constantly fighting wars against invaders or nearby kingdoms. The key to their power and success was the skill of their armies and their advanced weapons, including bows, axes and spears.

Besides moving fast, chariots gave the commanders extra height, so they could see the action and direct their armies.

The army was led by nobles or royals, who charged into battle on horse-drawn bronze chariots. Each chariot could carry up to three people – a driver, a warrior carrying a dagger-axe, and an archer. Archers had bronze-tipped arrows and strong bows.

The rest of the army was made up of foot soldiers, along with farmers and other commoners who could be called up when needed. The king and several other nobles each had their own armies and supplies of armour and weapons to use in war.

Shang culture

Besides farming, fighting and sacrificing, the Shang did a lot of creative and scientific things. They played music, wrote poetry, made art and studied the stars. The dynasty is also famous for its writing system.

Musical instruments

The brilliant bronze-work skills of the Shang meant they could make delicate, detailed musical instruments. They had bronze drums, cymbals, and bells with different notes which could be played by a group of musicians to make a tune. Besides using music for entertainment, it was probably used as part of religious rituals, and when marching into battle.

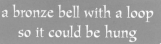
a bronze bell with a loop so it could be hung

a Shang dynasty drum made from sections of moulded bronze

Players taking part in a modern Go tournament in China.

Fact file: Games

Shang people may have passed the time by playing ancient board games, called Luibo and Go. According to legend, Go was invented in Xia dynasty times. It's still played today.

Writing it down

Shang writing is known as oracle bone script. It's found on bronze and jade objects, as well as on the oracle bones. The writings found so far mainly date from the Anyang period, but the script had probably developed over hundreds of years.

human

fish

ear

mountain

sun

moon

rain

Shang writing is made up of pictograms – little pictures that represent different things. In many of them you can see the picture clearly.

Fact file: Writing tools

To write on the oracle bones, a scribe had to carve the letters with a pointed bronze tool. They sometimes painted them on first with a brush, then carved out the shapes. It was a tricky job, and some of the bones have neater writing than others!

Astronomy

Shang scientists studied the stars, Sun and Moon, and used them to work out a calendar. It had 12 months of about 30 days each, divided into ten-day-long weeks. This added up to a year of about 360 days. As there are 365 days in a year – the time it takes for the Earth to **orbit** the Sun – each year was five days short. Every six years or so, the Shang added up these missing days to make a 30-day month and added this extra month to the year to catch up. So the Shang calendar is a repeated pattern of five years in a row of 12 months, about 360 days. Then one year of 13 months, about 390 days.

The calendar was important for deciding things like when to plant crops and make sacrifices.

Decoration and design

When archaeologists first uncovered Shang artefacts, they were amazed by the beautiful, detailed decoration on them.

Beautiful bronzes

Bronze was already an important metal in China before the Shang dynasty. It was associated with royalty, and owning bronze was a sign of wealth and power. The Shang continued this by making their bronze bowls, jars and pots as **intricate** and perfect as possible.

This bronze sculpture shows a crouching tiger with two tails, and a bird on its back.

Instead of beating or shaping the bronze, the Shang made clay moulds and filled them with the molten metal.

1 First, a model of the object and all the decoration on it, was formed from clay.

2 A hollow mould was made by pressing more clay around the model.

3 The mould was filled with liquid bronze, then picked off once the bronze had hardened.

Besides patterns and faces, the Shang loved using animal designs. Their bronzes featured many creatures such as elephants, dragons, tigers and birds.

Magical jade

Shang craftsmen included skilled carvers who made beautiful jade ornaments. This precious stone was highly valued in China, in the same way that gold is in some cultures. It was thought to have magical powers, protecting the person who owned it from harm, or even giving them **immortality**. For this reason the Shang also buried plenty of jade in royal tombs.

Jade is extremely hard. To shape it, carvers had to slowly wear it away by rubbing it with sand made from other, even harder stones. This took a long time, so carved jade objects were very valuable.

Smaller items like jewellery and figures were often carved from jade.

Fact file: Xi Wangmu

Xi Wangmu, or the Mother of the West, is an ancient Chinese goddess of time, space and stars. She's mentioned on one of the Shang oracle bones, and may have been one of their many gods. According to Chinese legends, she lived in a jade palace on a jade mountain.

Downfall of the dynasty

Just over 3,000 years ago, in 1046 BCE, the Shang dynasty finally came to an end, after more than 500 years of rule.

Just as the Shang had once seized power, another clan, the Zhou, grew strong enough to overthrow them.

The fall of the dynasty was largely blamed on the terrible behaviour of its last king, Di Xin.

This old illustration is said to show cruel King Di Xin and his wife Daji in their palace.

VIP file: Di Xin

King Di Xin's 29-year reign lasted from 1075 BCE to 1046 BCE. At first, he was a brave and clever king. But as time went on, he grew more and more greedy, selfish and cruel. Along with his wife Daji, he tortured and murdered people for entertainment. He demanded huge **taxes** from the commoners to pay for his luxurious palaces and parties. Most famously of all, he is said to have made a lake of wine with meat hanging from trees above it, for himself and his friends to feast on.

There are many bronze wine containers dating from late Shang times, showing wine was an important part of royal life.

King Wen's plan

The Zhou people were once loyal to the Shang kings, but fell out with them after the Shang killed their leader, King Ji. Ji's son, King Wen, **conquered** nearby lands to increase his power, and gathered a large Zhou army. With the help of his adviser, Jiang Ziya, he planned to attack the Shang.

However, King Wen died, and his son Wu became king of the Zhou. Jiang Ziya told Wu to wait until the Shang people were well and truly fed up of King Di Xin, before attacking. Finally, in 1046 BCE, Wu sent his army to **besiege** the city of Yin.

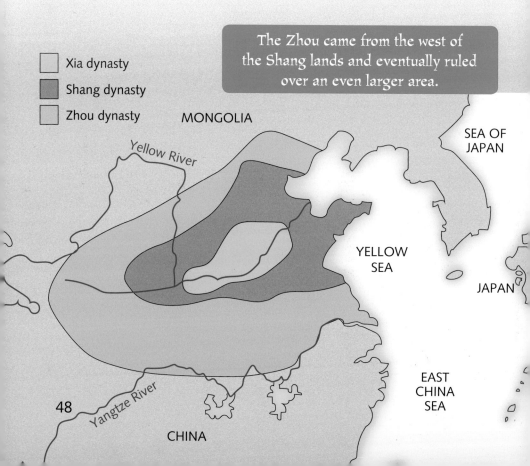

The Zhou came from the west of the Shang lands and eventually ruled over an even larger area.

Xia dynasty

Shang dynasty

Zhou dynasty

MONGOLIA

Yellow River

SEA OF JAPAN

YELLOW SEA

JAPAN

EAST CHINA SEA

Yangtze River

CHINA

48

VIP file: Jiang Ziya

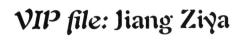

Jiang Ziya was once a Shang adviser, but he hated
King Di Xin so much that he escaped to the countryside.
According to Chinese historians, King Wen met Jiang
fishing by a river. He realised he was very wise and
asked him to help overthrow the Shang. Jiang's daughter
married King Wu, so he also became the king's
father-in-law.

The last battle

King Wu's army charged on Di Xin's forces in the great Battle of Muye, near Yin. Though Wu's army was smaller, many of Di Xin's soldiers hated him so much, they refused to fight for him, and went to join the Zhou side. King Wu was soon able to surround and conquer the city.

When Di Xin realised he'd been defeated, he locked himself in his palace, set it alight and died in the fire. The Zhou took over all the Shang lands, and expanded them into an even bigger empire.

Shang kings lead their armies in battle.

Legacy of the Shang

Though their dynasty didn't last forever, the Shang people lived on, ruled by other dynasties, and their culture had a great influence on China. The Chinese still use a calendar similar to the Shang's. Their writing system also became the basis of modern Chinese written characters.

Today, you can go and see Shang tombs and treasures for yourself at ancient sites in China and museums around the world.

Glossary

ancestors	family members who lived in the past
archaeologist	experts who study old buildings and objects to find out how people used to live
arrogant	behaving as though you're better than other people
decoded	to work out a code
BCE	stands for Before the Common Era
besiege	surround by soldiers in an attack
conquered	overcame by force
excavations	digs to find materials
exported	sent to another country to sell
fertile	good for growing crops
imitation	a copy of something else
immortality	living for ever
interpret	explain the meaning
intricate	with lots of detailed decoration
lavish	large and expensive
minister	politicians who help to govern a country
orbit	the curved path that a planet, satellite or spacecraft moves around another object in space
ramparts	strong, wide walls around a city or castle
rituals	set ways of going through religious ceremonies
sacrifices	acts of killing something or giving it up as an offering to a god or ancestor
scribe	a skilled worker whose job was to write things down
taxes	payments people make to a ruler or government

Index

Making a dynasty

in charge

home in the city

home in the countryside

food and drink

reading and writing

gods and sacrifice

arts and crafts

war

burials

Ideas for reading

Written by Clare Dowdall, PhD
Lecturer and Primary Literacy Consultant

Reading objectives:
- check that the book makes sense to them, discussing their understanding and exploring the meaning of words in context
- summarise the main ideas drawn from more than one paragraph, identifying key details that support the main ideas
- retrieve and record information from non-fiction

Spoken language objectives:
- participate in discussions, presentations, performances, role play, improvisations and debates

Curriculum links: History – early civilisations

Resources: ICT for research, art materials, writing materials, food and implements for a Shang feast.

Build a context for reading

- Show children the front cover and introduce the term "Dynasty". Ask children to suggest what it might mean, and to suggest synonyms (clan, family, tribe, group, etc.). Turn to the glossary to model how to look up new words.
- Read the blurb together. Discuss what life might have been like in England at the time the Shang existed to build children's awareness of the period. Check that children understand the acronym BCE (Before the Common Era) and what it means.
- Ask children what they can deduce about the Shang Dynasty based on the image on the front cover.

Understand and apply reading strategies

- Explain that you are going to read the first section aloud (pp2–3) and note the most important information.
- Ask a volunteer to read p4. Discuss what information is given and what can be deduced, e.g. the dates are given, but children can make deductions about why the Shang located its cities around the Yellow River.